Bridges

Written by Rod Rees
Series Consultant: Linda Hoyt

WorldWise
Content-based Learning

Contents

Introduction

Long ago, when people came to a wide and deep stream, how did they get across?

They made a simple bridge, usually from a log of wood. Simple bridges have always been made from **materials** that are easy to find. A log of wood across a stream can be a bridge.

Wood can also be used to make bigger bridges that last longer than simple bridges. Stone bridges are much stronger and last longer than wooden bridges.

But once people were able to **produce** iron and steel, they began building long, high, strong bridges that last a very long time.

Chapter 1
Building simple bridges

Footbridges

Bridges made from rope, **bamboo** or logs are built in places where these **materials** are easy to find. They are often built in forests.

Rope, bamboo and log bridges are strong enough to carry a few people at a time, but they are not strong enough to carry cars or heavier vehicles.

These footbridges may not last long. They can be burned in a fire or washed away in a flood.

Chapter 2
Building stronger bridges

Wooden bridges

Most wooden bridges are bigger and stronger than rope or **bamboo** bridges, and they can carry heavier traffic than small footbridges.

People have built all kinds of wooden bridges.

In some places, they have built covered wooden bridges to protect the wood from rain and help stop it from rotting.

But wooden bridges can also be destroyed by fire or washed away in a flood.

Stone bridges

Stone bridges are much stronger than bridges made from wood. They can be built across wide valleys or **waterways**, and can carry very heavy traffic. Some stone bridges were built hundreds of years ago and are still used today.

Stone bridges are often very beautiful. Stone can be cut into different shapes to make bridges that are both beautiful and interesting to look at.

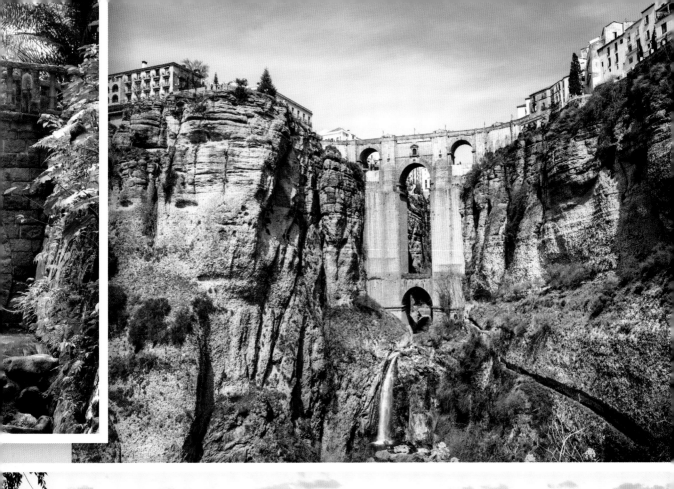

Iron and steel bridges

Bridges are also made from iron and steel. The first iron bridge was built around 200 years ago.

Most iron and steel bridges are longer, stronger and wider than wooden or stone bridges. They can carry much more traffic than most wooden or stone bridges because they have many lanes for cars, buses and trucks.

Sometimes, these bridges also have railroad tracks so that trains can cross them.

Iron and steel bridges help to move traffic around busy, crowded cities.

Chapter 3
Famous bridges

Some bridges are famous. People all around the world know about them.

There are very long bridges that reach across wide rivers, lakes or **harbours**. There are high bridges that are built across deep valleys or **gorges**.

There are bridges that can open up in the middle to allow ships and boats to pass underneath.

The Golden Gate Bridge in San Francisco took workers four years to build.

Stores and cafes were built along the Ponte Vecchio in Italy.

The Pont de Normandie connects two towns in France.

Verrazano Bridge

Very long bridges

The Verrazano Bridge is the longest **suspension** bridge in the United States and was once the longest bridge in the world. This famous bridge is very important because it joins New York City to Staten Island and Brooklyn.

The bridge has two levels and carries thirteen lanes of traffic.

Did you know?

Nearly 200,000 vehicles cross the Verrazano Bridge each day.

Very high bridges

The Sydney Harbour Bridge is
one of the tallest arch bridges
in the world. People can walk
or drive across it and there
are also two lanes for trains to
travel over it. Many tourists
who come to Sydney, travel
over the bridge to see the
amazing views of the harbour.

The Sydney Harbour Bridge is built high above
the water so that ships can pass underneath.

A bridge that opens

Tower Bridge in London, England, is a bridge that opens. It is made from stone and steel, and it took eight years to build. Tower Bridge opens in the middle to let large boats travel up and down the River Thames.

Tower Bridge

Conclusion

There are many different kinds of bridges. People can ride, walk, drive or go by train across bridges. Boats can travel under some bridges.

Many bridges – some of them old and some of them new – are so amazing that they are famous around the world.

Glossary

bamboo a tall plant with a hard, hollow stem

gorges narrow valleys with steep walls

harbours protected parts of a lake or sea that are safe for boats

materials things that are used to make other things

produce to make something

suspension a type of bridge that hangs by cables that are held up by towers

waterways bodies of water such as rivers and canals that boats can travel along

Index